Our Seven Principles
in Story and Verse

A Collection for Children and Adults

Kenneth W. Collier

Skinner House Books
Boston

Published by Skinner House Books, an imprint of the Unitarian
Universalist Association, 25 Beacon Street, Boston, MA 02108-2800.

ISBN 1-55896-353-7

Printed in Canada.

10 9 8 7 6 5 4 3 2
00 99

For Anne
who helps me in more ways than she knows

Contents

Introduction

I have been a Unitarian Universalist minister for more than fifteen years. Visitors and new members to my congregation often ask, "What do Unitarian Universalists believe?" I struggle with that question. Even people who have been Unitarian Universalists most, or all, of their lives struggle with this question. Obviously we believe something. We are, after all, a coherent religious body. But *what* do we believe? What makes us Unitarian Universalists?

Sometimes I hear silly answers like, "Because we Unitarian Universalists don't have a creed, a set of dogmas, or a confession of faith, we don't believe anything," or "We can believe anything we want"—which is just another way of saying we don't believe anything. If this were true, then it would follow that we Unitarian Universalists do not believe anything *as Unitarian Universalists*. And if we believe nothing as Unitarian Universalists, then anything would be as good as anything else and there would be no coherence, no identity, no sense of ourselves as Unitarian Universalists. And that is clearly not the case.

All too often I hear Unitarian Universalists say, "Well, I don't know what I *do* believe, but I certainly do *not* believe . . ."—you can fill in the blank with your favorite non-belief. We think it is enough to be negative without ever being positive. Not only is this a terrible way to define or even characterize something, but, far worse, it is an incredibly effective way of being stuck in rejection and denial and preventing spiritual and intellectual growth. If it is true that we do not stand for anything or believe anything or that we can believe anything we want, Unitarian Universalists would be just another bunch of confused people milling around without center or edges or substance. And if we can do no better than tell people what we do not believe, then none of us would discover the beauty and integrity of who we are. All we would have to offer would be the negativity of who and what we are not. And why would anyone be interested in knowing that?

I do not want to suggest that we always are or could be articulate about the Profound Integrity within our hearts or our central and defining beliefs. As the early twentieth-century Viennese philosopher Ludwig Wittgenstein remarked, "We finally reach a point at which all we can do is make inarticulate noise." But it is important that we grapple with the core from time to time and be able to say something positive about it. It is important for all of us to be able to say, "This I believe. This I stand for. This is who I am and this is what moves me forward." And we should be willing to say this even while knowing that any statement we make is provisional, subject to change, growth, and development as we continue to grapple with the core. The reflections in this book are a record of some of my wrestling.

So, what do we believe? We believe that each human being contains a reservoir of Deep Integrity or Profound Beauty, and that our religious lives begin when we encounter that Inviolable Profundity within our hearts and souls. But this is something that has to be done as an individual. The idea of individuality is complicated and confusing. There is no such thing as an individual apart from a community. Yet we act as individuals and we think and feel and emote in a kind of isolation from each other. No one can think my thoughts; no one can feel my emotions or sensations; no one could experience my birth or death. It is in this sense that we experience the Holy alone in the pristine and profound integrity of our individual hearts. This, we maintain, is the beginning of religion.

This experience is often a non-verbal experience, and because each of us is unique, each of us comes from the experience with a unique understanding of what the experience was and what its object was, what it moves us to do and how we understand it. Each of us articulates the experience differently. Ours is a religious movement in which we treasure and cultivate these differences. It is less important to us that we reach agreement with each other on theological matters than that we stimulate each other to deeper thinking and understanding. The result is that we do not have *a* single theology. We have a whole spectrum of *theologies*, some of which are a little difficult to understand as *theo*logy.

All of this brings us up rather short when someone asks, "What do Unitarian Universalists believe?" What is there to say? We have no creed, no confession of faith, no body of dogma, and we disagree a lot about theological matters. There are few statements I can appeal to that most Unitarian Universalists will agree with—at least few that are worth bothering with. There is one exception, though, and that is the statement of Principles and Purposes in the Bylaws of the Unitarian Universalist Association. This is something that is both agreed upon among us generally and says something worth listening to and contemplating. The Principles read as follows:

We, the member congregations of the Unitarian Universalist Association, covenant to affirm and promote:

- The inherent worth and dignity of every person;
- Justice, equity, and compassion in human relations;
- Acceptance of one another and encouragement to spiritual growth in our congregations;
- A free and responsible search for truth and meaning;
- The right of conscience and the use of the democratic process within our congregations and in society at large;

4

- The goal of world community with peace, liberty, and justice for all;
- Respect for the interdependent web of all existence of which we are a part.

The living tradition we share draws from many sources:

- Direct experience of that transcending mystery and wonder, affirmed in all cultures, which moves us to a renewal of the spirit and an openness to the forces that create and uphold life;
- Wisdom and deeds of prophetic women and men which challenge us to confront powers of evil with justice, compassion, and the transforming power of love;
- Wisdom from the world's religions which inspires us in our ethical and spiritual lives;
- Jewish and Christian teachings which call us to respond to God's love by loving our neighbors as ourselves;
- Humanist teachings which counsel us to heed the guidance of reason and the results of science, and warn us against idolatries of the mind and spirit;
- Spiritual teachings of Earth-centered traditions which celebrate the sacred circle of life and instruct us to live in harmony with the rhythms of nature.

Grateful for the religious pluralism which enriches and ennobles our faith, we are inspired to deepen our understanding and expand our vision. As free congregations, we enter into this convent, promising to one another our mutual trust and support.

For years, when a new member asked me "The Question," I used to give them a copy of the Principles, but this would only stimulate more questions. I decided in 1994 to preach a series of sermons based on the seven Principles. As I got into my project, it occurred to me that these sermons would be a good thing to give new people who want to know what Unitarian Universalists believe. It would even make interesting reading for longtime Unitarian Universalists who want to see how a minister wrestles with these issues.

In addition to my sermons, which have been recast as essays for reading, this book contains poetry and stories, one poem and one story for each principle. There are two reasons for this. Most of my sermons were delivered on Sundays when children in my congregation attended the first part of the service, so I decided to write stories for them that would express the principle of that Sunday. In my services I also used poems that I had written for the occasion. These poems form a kind of personal credo, a statement of my own beliefs, and it seemed appropriate to include them here. What you have in this book are three different ways that I have thought about, wrestled with, and expressed my beliefs about the seven Principles. I hope they stimulate you in your own religious life and thinking.

I wrote all of the stories in this book, but I have borrowed themes from various cultures. The first story, "Yammani and the Soji," is based on Jesus' parable of the Good Samaritan (Luke 10: 29-37). I've always thought that this story is one of the most important in the entire New Testament. Indeed, it can be argued that it is an encapsulation of his entire message, spiritual as well as social. The problem with this story is that few people understand its original context, so they tend to miss its power and importance. I've tried to solve that problem by recasting it in its entirety.

The origin of "The Dog and the Heartless King" is lost in the mists of time and the folklore of India. I found a version of it in *From Long Ago and Many Lands,* by Sophia Lyon Fahs. My story rewrites Fahs's version. The stories "How Coyote Lost His Songs, Music, and Dance," "Hare's Gifts," and "How Spider Woman Created the World" borrow idioms from Native America and Africa, though all three are my own stories.

"The Hidden Treasure of Lvov" was originally an Hassidic story, but I cannot remember where I first encountered it. It may have been in one of Elie Wiesel's books, or in a volume of Martin Buber's *Tales of the Hassidim.* In any event, the story stuck with me, and when I began to think about the fourth Principle, I remembered it. At one level, it does not matter where I first encountered it because this version is told through the filter of my own thinking and life. At another level, I would like to give credit where credit is due.

Making a story one's own is the difference between a living story and a dead one. A living story is told and re-told and changes and grows; a dead story is told over and over, each time exactly like the last. A living story changes with the storyteller; a dead story never changes. A living story is not owned by anyone but belongs to everyone and has to grow into the lives of those who hear it; a dead story belongs to the "Critical Edition." You cannot really copyright a living story, because it does not belong to you any more than your children belong to you.

"Shirley's Story" is unapologetically autobiographical. I used it originally on a Sunday when I wanted to talk about racism and was unable to think up a story that made the following point: racism is not just something abstract that adults talk about. It is concrete—so concrete that it wrenches and destroys the real lives of real people. The more I thought about it, the more it seemed that the best way I could make that point real was to tell the story of how I began to discover the terrible truth about racism.

I offer you, then, three versions of my reflections on basic Unitarian Universalism. Longtime Unitarian Universalists may find it interesting to see how near or far we are from each other in our articulation of basic, shared religious ideas. I would be pleased to hear from you— questions, critiques, suggestions, your reflections, or anything else. Newcomers to Unitarian Universalism may find it interesting to see how I have tried to answer "The Question" in some depth. I would be pleased to hear from you, too. The essence of growth is interaction, and nothing would please me more than for this book to become the stimulus for people interacting with each other, and so growing.

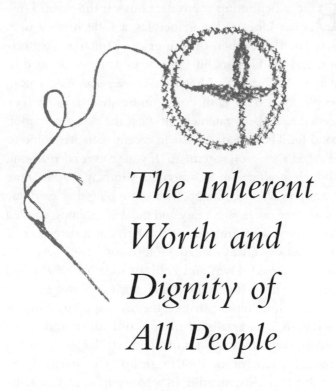

The Inherent Worth and Dignity of All People

Before beginning my reflections on the seven Unitarian Universalist Principles, a little history is in order. In 1961, when the American Unitarian Association and the Universalist Church in America decided to merge and form the Unitarian Universalist Association, people from both faith communities realized that they needed to make a statement of what the new Association stood for. They needed what in recent years has come to be called a "mission statement." If you've ever been around a bunch of Unitarian Universalists, you may wonder how it was possible to come up with something that everyone could agree on. It wasn't easy, and the debate almost scuttled the whole effort. But out of the ferment a statement of principles was finally crafted. Unfortunately, this statement was so watered down and cobbled together that it had only one virtue: It permitted merger to go through.

Over time, feminism became an important part of Unitarian Universalist thinking and more and more women were dissatisfied with the sexist language in the original statement. In 1980, a group of Unitarian Universalist feminists, meeting in a convention in East Lansing, Michigan, looked carefully at the original Unitarian Universalist Principles and realized that not only were they riddled with sexist language, they were also ill-conceived, badly written, and insubstantial. They began a process that culminated in 1985 with the formal adoption of a new statement of principles that is carefully thought out, well written, and has substance.

This statement is not a creed; it is not a set of dogmas or a confession of faith. It is not even something that we agree on with unanimity or that we always manage to live up to. It is just a set of basic principles, rather like the document "Things Commonly Believed Among Us" adopted in 1894 by what was then the Western Unitarian Conference. No one is bound to the language of the Unitarian Universalist Principles to be a Unitarian Universalist; no one is required to believe all of these things to be a Unitarian Universalist; no one will be excluded from the circle of our fellowship because of any disagreement with this document. But because most of us are willing to assent at least to most of it, it provides a good beginning for us to examine our beliefs, a ground from which to begin.

We do not always manage to live up to the rhetoric in our Principles. This is not only to be expected, but as it should be. What kind of Principles would they be if they were so easy to live up to that they do not call us, challenge us, pull us forward into an ever-growing and -deepening way of living? One of the characteristics of contemporary Unitarian Universalism is that we believe religious life is on-going and developing.

Unitarian Universalists are not afraid of doubt in, or failure to live up to, our Principles, because we believe that any statement of belief is transient, at most an approximation of something permanent and too deep to ever be fully articulated or expressed in human life. The religious task is always in process. When we fail to live up to our rhetoric, we do not see that failure as a fault or the result of an inherent evil within ourselves, but as an indication of our inherent human limitations. Recognition of failure is not a cause for breast beating but for healing and moving toward something deeper and fuller. It is not a pretext for blame but an opportunity to become more fully human.

Telos is a concept in ancient Greek philosophy. It is a consummation, a completion, or a goal being striven for. The *telos* is that which draws something forward, that which gives a process its impetus and direction. It is what allows development to happen. Aristotle listed *telos* as one of the causes of things. A statement of religious principles is a kind of moral and spiritual *telos.* Even though we may not always manage to live fully in their light, they are what we strive for, what we aim at, what give us a sense of our unfolding as spiritual beings, which is another reason why it is important to come to some understanding of what we, as individuals, as a church, and as a religious movement, stand for. When people ask what Unitarian Universalists believe, they are asking what our *telos* is, how we understand it and grapple with it and allow it to give us definition, shape, and substance.

Consider, then, the first of these Principles: that we affirm and promote the inherent worth and dignity of every person. It does not say the inherent worth and dignity of people with whom we happen to agree or whom we like. It says every person. It does not say the inherent worth and dignity of like-minded people, or people who are willing to enter into rational, civilized discourse with us. It does not say people with whom we may disagree but who are honorable and as genuine in their beliefs as we are in ours. It says *every* person. We are also called to affirm the inherent worth and dignity of people whom we thoroughly dislike, people whom we find obnoxious, obstreperous, overbearing, and frightening; people whom we find abhorrent and whose beliefs and behavior we find disgusting; even people who would deny, silence, or destroy us. This principle calls on us to affirm and promote the inherent worth and dignity of *every person*, and it does not admit exceptions.

This is a tall order. "Every person" includes the people we love and the people we dislike. It includes the oppressed and the oppressor. It includes the victim and the perpetrator. It includes the Jews of Central Europe as well as Hitler. It includes the bully down the street who terrorized us when we were children. It includes the child molester, the battering husband, the abusive alcoholic, the drug dealer, the crack house operator, and the gang members. It includes everyone.

Does anyone really believe that inherent worth and dignity dwell within every person? If so, how can it be promoted even in terrible people? I, for one, believe that worth and dignity cannot be snuffed out no matter what a person may do in his or her life. Worth and dignity are absolute in the sense that they are independent of what happens to us or what we may do in our lives. Any religion that calls on me to be respectful where respect is easy, but lets me off the hook when it is difficult, is not worth bothering with. Such a religion will never challenge me to grow or deepen or become more fully human. I reject any religion that does not make me squirm occasionally when I consider my behavior, or that does not call me to grow toward those things that I need to be. I reject any religion that is not a *telos*.

What I have called the Profoundly Beautiful lives deep within the heart of every human being. This Profound Beauty is the spiritual foundation of life; the religious task is to make the Profound visible in our lives, to lend it our flesh that it may be incarnate. It is no more possible to lose this spiritual foundation than to lose our genetic foundation. It *is* possible to lose sight of our own profundity. It *is* possible to blind ourselves to it, to ignore it, to forsake it, to fail to believe in it, to exclude it from the reality of our living. It *is* possible to refuse the religious task and deny the Profound Beauty of one's own life. But it is not possible to lose it. It is there at birth, at death, and at every moment in between. It is by virtue of this Profound Beauty that every human being is inherently valuable and dignified no matter what is done with the life that one is given.

Sometimes it is easy to affirm and promote the worth and dignity of others and sometimes it is very difficult, but it is always required. In 1994, the 125th anniversary of the birth of Mohandas K. Gandhi was celebrated. One of the reasons why he was such a great person, called in Hindi a *Mahatma* or Great Soul, is that he lived and struggled without ever losing sight of the profundity within himself and all human beings. The greatness of his soul was a reflection of the greatness of all souls, and he kept his attention on the Greatness of Soul, drawing on the strength of the inherent worth and dignity of all, for he knew that his worth and dignity was neither more nor less than the British, against whom he struggled.

Sometimes affirmation and promotion require nothing more than listening and agreeing, or no more than a friendly disagreement, an intellectual conversation. Sometimes it requires me to hold myself in respectful opposition to someone and to speak truths that are painful to others or myself. Sometimes it requires me to hold people accountable for their actions, and sometimes it requires me to do things that are difficult and painful but ultimately healing. Sometimes it requires that I go in harm's way and take risks for myself and others. Sometimes it even requires me to hurt someone. And probably more often than I like to admit, it requires me to change my behavior, my way of living, my way of thinking about things. It requires me to admit that I have been wrong.

The following story, "Yammani and the Soji," is a version of Jesus' story of the Good Samaritan. Jesus had been asked which of all the laws in the Torah is the most important, and he singles out two: that we love God and that we love our neighbor. In Luke's Gospel, Jesus was then asked about the second law. Who are our neighbors? His answer was the Good Samaritan story. It illustrates his point because it is the hated Samaritan rather than the pious Judeans who is able to see beyond divisions that separate people. He alone respected the worth and dignity of the injured man and helped him. "Yammani and the Soji" makes the same point because it is a hated Soji rather than a respected villager who understands that need is real and shared but difference is an illusion. He alone understands and respects the worth and dignity of the orphaned child.

There is a word for this action in classical Christian theology: redemption. It is not a word that one often hears in Unitarian Universalist churches. In classical Christianity, we are redeemed by Jesus' sacrifice. To be redeemed is to be bought back, as it were, from sin and its consequences by Jesus' death and resurrection. Though I would use the word, I would not use it in this sense. Another meaning of "redemption" is "to fulfill a promise." The promise is of worth and dignity, the Profound Beauty that dwells within us all.

It is as if we make a promise at birth, a promise to fulfill, to bring to life, to realize the Profound Beauty that is within us and makes us miraculous things. Our spiritual lives are nothing more nor less than our coming to understand that Profound Beauty more deeply and clearly, and fulfilling—redeeming—the promise in every action that we do. As far as I can tell, I cannot recognize the worth and dignity within myself unless I also recognize it everywhere I may look, even in people within whom it is dark and hidden, rejected and forgotten—like the Soji. As far as I fail to recognize the Profound Beauty in another, I fail to see it clearly in myself. As far as I deny it in another, I deny it in myself. The extent to which I affirm it in myself, I must affirm it wherever I look, for, as every religious genius who has ever lived has affirmed, the center of the universe is everywhere, not least in the hearts of every human being.

Do I succeed in this? Sometimes. But it is the *telos* that drives my life. It is the standard against which I measure myself, the guideline, the principle, the goal. And one of the reasons I am a Unitarian Universalist is precisely because this idea, however it may be stated, is and always has been part of our unfolding, living heritage, both the Unitarian and the Universalist. It has never been watered down. It has always called us to the very best and most exacting standard: to redeem the promise of our birth by giving our flesh to the Profound and to call it forth from all human beings.

Yammani and the Soji

It was the first day of the Festival of Purification. All the rites and ceremonies had been celebrated and the people purified, the stain of the sins of the old year washed away so that they might approach the coming year with pure hearts and clean minds. All the village had gathered at the Great Hall for feasting and dancing—and especially for the stories. This year the great storyteller Yammani had come to their village for the festival. Everyone had gathered—that is everyone except the Soji clan, who were fit only for necessary but demeaning work such as burying the dead and disposing waste.

The people owned no slaves, for they believed that all must be free to live the lives that the gods had granted them. But there were still certain, distasteful tasks that had to be done, and few people would voluntarily do these things. And so, from time out of mind, the members of the Soji clan had been forced to do them. No one knew any longer why or how it had come about, but the Soji and no one else buried the dead and collected the garbage and spread manure on the fields and did the other unclean work. And because they did these things, no one in the village had anything to do with them—unless to give orders. Most people would not even touch a Soji, or if they did, by accident or through necessity, they would go to the river immediately and wash thoroughly.

That night the feast went on and on until all in the village were satisfied, even the few wanderers who happened to be there. Then the dancing began, with its music and beguilingly graceful movements. But even the most graceful body tires eventually, and in time the music stilled and the dancers sat to rest. Then all eyes turned to Yammani, who had been strangely silent all evening.

"So, Yammani," said the Chief of the Elders, rising and turning to her. "You have come into our village this year, and the time has come for us to hear your story."

"So it has," Yammani replied. "So it has. What story would you have me tell? Shall it be a story of the gods or a story of the people?"

"Tell us a story of how the people may approach the gods, for this is the Festival of Purification."

All evening Yammani had seemed to be brooding, as though she was trying to decide how to tell these people the story they most needed to hear. At this suggestion, her eyes brightened, for she knew what to do.

"There was once a family who lived on their farm in the mountains. Their life was one of hard work, but it was sweet enough. Once every year they came in from the farm to sell their crops and buy the tools and other goods that they needed for the coming year. This particular year, the crops were harvested and the family set out as usual for the town. On the way, they were attacked by bandits. All men were murdered and the women and children were taken to be sold as slaves or worse on some far country. The only one to escape was a small child, about six years old, who was hidden by its mother and overlooked in the confusion.

"As it happened, the attack was near a village much like this one. The child, driven by hunger, afraid and crying, made its way into the center where many people had gathered in the market that afternoon. The Chief of the Elders was there, but he was so deeply involved in village affairs that he did not notice one more crying child, even though he passed right by it. Many parents were there and they all heard the child, for what parent does not hear a child crying? Many thought that someone ought to help this poor, frightened child, but all were too busy, too hurried or harried, or had barely enough for their own.

"Toward the end of the day, a Soji came to clean out the stalls of the donkeys and the cattle. When this Soji heard the child crying, he stopped his work to look for it. He held the child and comforted it and dried its tears. And when he found out what had happened, he who had so little and was constantly worried about food for his own children, brought this child into his home and loved it and cared for it and raised it as his own."

In the silence, Yammani turned to the Chief of the Elders and asked, "In this village, who approached the gods?"

The Elder cast his eyes to the floor, but Yammani demanded an answer with her burning eyes. Finally the Chief of the Elders whispered, "the Soji."

"Yes. It was the Soji," said Yammani, holding the stillness around her. "It was the Soji." And so saying, she swept out of the village to spend the rest of her life among the Soji.

The Chalice of the Heart

A mother holds her baby to her breast and smiles,
And her baby stares deeply into her eyes.
He reaches his hand lightly up to her ebony chest;
He lies in her dark arms, bathed in love that runs
Like warm, sweet milk filling his round belly,
Filling his growing heart, flowing into him
Yet never emptying the chalice of her heart.

Two gray-haired lovers walk beside the sea,
Hand in hand, like a couple of teenagers,
Lost in the silent language of hands
And glowing eyes and hearts beating together,
Lost in the silent, mysterious language
That speaks the pain of the heart and heals.
Two loving women walk beside the sea.

There is a light that burns in the chalice of the heart,
And so powerful is that light that it illuminates the soul
And sparkles in the mind and dances in the eye.
One ray of this light can leap from the heart,
Can join with another, can reveal the mystery of love.
For worth knows worth, and light knows light,
And love dances between heart and heart.

Even though darkness deepens without end,
Leaches into the heart, reaches poisoned fingers

To snuff the light and murder the flame,
To still the dance and blind the sparkling eye,
I believe that the light will never go out;
I believe that the chalice cannot be emptied;
I believe that love emerges from dignity,
And merges with dignity and returns in dignity.

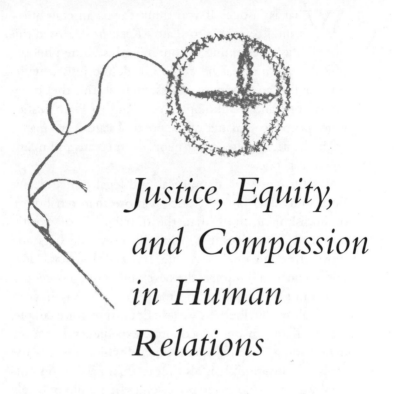

*Justice, Equity,
and Compassion
in Human
Relations*

What is justice? If you think this is an easy question, I refer you to Plato's *Republic*. He used this question as a beginning for outlining his entire philosophy, discovering that he could not define justice without paying attention to issues such as the theory of knowledge and psychology. According to Plato, justice is not primarily a matter of the political state. It is a matter of the heart, for only a just people can create and maintain a just state.

In this sense, social, political, and legal justice derive from individual justice. Justice is more than retribution or punishment, more than the distribution of wealth, power, and prestige. It is primarily how one lives and moves through one's own life. If a political state does not maintain and support the development of just people, it will not be a just state no matter how it may treat its criminals or distribute its wealth. Education, for example, is more than a matter of economic expediency. It is more than reading, writing, and arithmetic, which are only the tools of education. It is also more than passing on cultural values like so many poker chips. If a child passively receives cultural values like a sponge and cannot do anything with them, that child has not received an education. True education is a matter of creating human beings, people whose depth, worth, and dignity are respected, supported, and developed as fully as possible so that they do not simply receive culture but create it as a living tradition. Thus education is a matter of justice.

What does it mean to be a just person? According to Plato, to be a just person is to have a certain balance of the principles of the soul. I understand this answer to mean that a just person has achieved a kind of inner peace, an ordering of oneself within, a recognition and acceptance of one's worth, and a cultivation of dignity.

Carl Gustav Jung likened neurosis to an internal civil war, a person in conflict with himself or herself. Plato's ideal just person is one who has solved inner conflicts, ordered the heart, and is at peace. Black Elk, the Oglala Holy Man says that there are three kinds of peace: that which is within the heart, that which is between friends and neighbors, and that which is among nations. But without peace within the heart there cannot be peace between neighbors or among nations. Peace cannot be maintained among people who are at war with themselves. The just have found peace within the heart and use that inner peace to live in harmony with their neighbors.

Justice in this sense is like genuine deep peace, not something that ordinary people can achieve in any final and finished way. It is a *telos,* a goal that moves us forward in the struggle to become deeper and more fully human. We are not just; we are becoming just.

Can someone who has achieved a reasonable level of justice within his or her soul treat others in an unequal way? Can such a person live in and tolerate inequality? Could such a person live in a village that contains Soji?

(See "Yammani and the Soji" in the first section.) It seems obvious that the answer is no. Justice requires a recognition that none is more valuable than another. How can someone cultivate his or her own dignity and fail to recognize the dignity of others? How can someone accept his or her own worth and value and deny that same value in others? In short, justice implies equity.

Lucy Stone was a Unitarian who fought courageously her entire life for the cause of equity, among other things. Unitarian Universalists are proud of her and others like her in our history, both the famous and the unknown, the men and women, clergy and lay, who worked, always courageously, sometimes silently and without recognition, for the day when equity could be taken for granted as part of our human heritage.

There were important and powerful Unitarian Universalist abolitionists and Suffragists. Some lived to see the abolition of slavery become a reality. Some lived to see women finally able to vote and some, like Lucy Stone, did not. There were Unitarian Universalists in the struggle for humane treatment of the mentally ill, and there were Unitarian Universalists on the Freedom Rides in Alabama and Mississippi. There have been Unitarian Universalists in almost every struggle for the equal and humane treatment of human beings, and we are very proud of our record in the struggle for equity.

Unfortunately, the struggle is not over. As soon as slavery was abolished in its most overt form, it was reinstituted in more subtle forms. The deeper issues were racism and class hatred and the unequal distribution of wealth, opportunity, and power, which we still struggle with. And this list is not complete. To it we have to add sexism, heterosexism and homophobia, ageism, ableism, and a whole host of behaviors and attitudes for which there is no name, but which prevent people from understanding that all are equal in worth, dignity, and inherent moral and spiritual value.

Perhaps you wonder at my use of the word "understanding." I do not mean "giving verbal or even intellectual assent." I mean a kind of existential grasp and commitment. As the word itself implies, to understand something in this sense is to "stand under" it, to live in the light of it. I know far too many people who readily say that they believe in justice, equity, and compassion, but this assent never breaks through to their hearts and changes their behavior. It is far less important to me what sounds come out of people's mouths than what words people speak in their hearts, for it is the words of the heart that change people's lives and direct their behavior and heal the brokenness of living.

The words of the heart cannot lie. You cannot speak in your heart what you do not believe, for this is genuine belief. The understanding of the heart, the words spoken within the integrity of who you are, these are the words and the understanding that guide people's lives. This is what is difficult and sometimes painful, and this is what I am talking about when I speak of understanding the equity of worth, dignity, and moral and spiritual value. This existential understanding of equity is what is needed if we are ever to live up to the example of the Lucy Stones of our history.

Equity, not as an external quality but as an existential commitment, is the understanding that no one is privileged and that the worth, value, and dignity of each person is as important and as sacred as one's own. How do we come to that understanding? Black Elk tells us that it is by coming to peace within our own hearts and souls. Jung tells us that it is by stilling the civil war within. Plato tells us that it is by becoming just within our hearts. This existential understanding is the soul of the primary sense of justice. Justice and equity are twins, justice being the internal state and equity being the manifestation of internal commitment.

How can I think that I or anyone else is more valuable or privileged if I am at peace with the reality of who I am? I have a faith, a deep trust, that the deeper I come to understand who I am and what is required of me to achieve the healing of my own heart, the deeper I will understand that there is no healing in the hurting of another. There is no peace in the breaking of another. There is no justice in the cheating of another. There is no worth in one save in the worth of all. There is no healing save in the healing of all. The more clearly and deeply I understand my own integrity, the more fully I understand that we are all bound together in a single beautiful and holy unity. In short, there is no justice without equity and there is no equity without compassion.

And so we come to compassion, one of the most misunderstood terms in religion. Today, the word "passion" means such things as boundless desire, intense sexual attraction, enormous enthusiasm and energy. "Passion" originally meant "suffering." It comes into the English language from a Proto-Indo-European root that means "to hurt." This same root also gives a Germanic word that means "to hate," and that Germanic word comes into English as "fiend." "Com-" is a prefix that comes from the Latin word *con*, which means "with." "Compassion," then, really means "to suffer with another."

It does not mean "to take away the suffering of another" or "to make it all better." Sometimes we can do that, and sometimes we cannot. But we can suffer together. We can share pain with another. We can identify with each other so strongly that when another person suffers, we can share that suffering. A couple of years ago at Thanksgiving, I learned the story of a young Lakota woman who heard about the suffering of certain children during a drought in Africa. She felt the need to do something for them, but being poor herself, she realized that she could not contribute anything material that would make the smallest dent in their suffering. Instead, she decided to fast for several days. Asked

33

why, she said that though she had nothing much to give to them, "at least I can share their suffering."

Compassion is about going beyond the sometimes defeatist and selfish thinking that says we are so isolated from each other that no one can touch, appreciate, or commune with another. When we think that we stop at our skin, compassion really does become impossible. But when we begin to understand—in an existential sense—that through love we can extend ourselves beyond the boundary of the skin, then compassion becomes not just possible, but the first expression of both equity and justice.

Let's look at the story of the Good Samaritan. What is the point of this story? People have argued over that one for years, and some of you may disagree with me. The way I read the story, it is about everything that I have been discussing. Every religion I know has some version of this story and says the same thing about it. The words you utter, the sounds you make, have little to do with whether or not you make peace in your heart, achieve eternal life, realize salvation, walk with the Tao, or become enlightened. What matters are the words you utter with your heart, within your soul. This is what condemns or saves. And the primary word that the soul utters is love.

The Buddha taught that the primary fruit of enlightenment is an all-embracing love, a love that holds such compassion for the suffering in the world that the enlightened one will sometimes vow to postpone entry into

Nirvana until all sentient beings are also enlightened. This is love and compassion. It is the foundation for the truth that we are, at the very deepest levels, one. I do not mean that we are numerically one, that I and other people are materially the same thing. Nor am I embracing what is known in philosophy as solipsism, the doctrine that the only thing that exists in the world is my own consciousness. I believe that although we are separate materially and in our consciousness, we are morally, religiously, and spiritually one. It is through love that we come to understand this and give it our deepest commitment.

How can we believe in equity, the idea that all are of equal moral and spiritual value, worth, and dignity, yet fail to show compassion to each other? How can we claim to support the cause of justice and search ever deeper for peace, internally and externally, and fail to show compassion for one another? How can we be compassionate except in love? How can we love one another and fail to grasp the spiritual unity that flows like a river through all of life? And how can we love and yet hold some to be more worthy than others? How can we uphold the inherent worth and dignity of all and fail to support justice, equity, and compassion?

And so I say that the primary word the soul utters is love. The source of justice as inner peace, of equity as existential commitment, and of compassion as the ability to suffer with another, is simply love. This love is nothing but understanding the inherent worth and dignity of all people. The second Unitarian Universalist Principle—the commitment to justice, equity, and compassion—is but the expression of the first. Justice, equity, and compassion are different names for the same thing, and that thing is love.

The Dog and the Heartless King

There was once a king who thought that everyone should always do exactly what he said and that he didn't have to care about anyone else. After all, he was the king. What did he care about anyone else? Even the people of his kingdom. What did he care? They existed only to serve his needs—or so he thought.

As a result of his selfish ideas, everyone in his kingdom was poor—except him. He had more money than even he needed, but he got his wealth by imposing huge taxes on his people and he never gave anything back. He did not build schools or hospitals or repair the roads. Instead he maintained enormous armies and built huge palaces for himself. Meanwhile, the people became poorer and poorer, and hungrier and hungrier, and more and more miserable. But the king didn't care. He had his, so why should he care about his people?

One day, the gods saw what was happening and decided to teach the king a lesson. They sent Lord Krishna in the form of a hunter, who came to the king offering him a gift: an enormous hunting dog. Now, the king enjoyed hunting—he had an enormous stable of horses and lots of dogs. But this dog was different, somehow. It was the biggest dog the king had ever seen. It was even big enough to hunt tigers! So he accepted the gift.

As soon as the king accepted the dog, it began to bark. Now, this dog's bark was not an ordinary bark. It was so loud that it actually shook the palace walls. And it wouldn't stop barking. It barked and barked and no one could stop it.

"What's wrong with your dog?" the king shouted to the hunter.

"He's not my dog. He's your dog," the hunter shouted back, "and he's hungry."

"No problem," shouted the king, and he ordered the servants to bring as much food as the dog could eat. But no matter how much food was brought, the dog gobbled it up and continued barking. As you can imagine, the king was not happy.

"Take your dog back and leave this kingdom immediately!" the king ordered.

"I can't. He's not my dog," the hunter replied. "Besides, I've been sent here by those who are greater and far more powerful than you. You're stuck with it."

The king started to be frightened. "What can I give the dog to satisfy him?"

"Only one thing will satisfy this dog," said the hunter. "So long as its enemies are loose in the kingdom, it will be hungry and will keep barking."

"No problem," said the king. "Who are his enemies?"

"His enemies are those who keep the people of this kingdom hungry. They are those who are taking most of the kingdom's food and don't leave enough for the people, the parents and children, the elderly, the sick. They are those who take all the people's money and do nothing with it. The children cannot learn in school, for there are no schools. The sick simply die in the streets because there are no hospitals. And all the while these greedy people simply get richer and richer while the people get poorer and poorer. As long as this keeps up, this dog will continue to bark. Get used to it."

The king was terrified at this, because he knew that the hunter was talking about him. It had never occurred to him that he was doing anything wrong. How could he be doing anything that would displease the gods? He was the king. He called in all of his advisors and councilors and asked them what could be done. They tried to think of something, but because of the racket from the dog's barking they couldn't think. They told the king that the only thing to be done was to feed the people, build schools and hospitals, and repair the roads.

Well, by now the king had realized that since this was no ordinary dog, this could be no ordinary hunter. It must be Lord Krishna. And that convinced him. He ordered his servants to open his barns and warehouses and granaries and to go through the kingdom feeding the hungry. He opened his treasuries and used the gold to build schools and hospitals and roads and he sent his own advisors out into the kingdom to teach and heal the people.

This took a lot of time and all that time the dog continued to bark. But at last the day came when the people were no longer hungry and every village had a school and a hospital. And when that day came, the dog stopped barking and lay down quietly at the king's feet. Everyone was happy and at peace with themselves and with their neighbors. And the king had learned his lesson.

The World Is a Single Place

I look out my window;
I walk through the hills;
I lose my mind in the mountains,
Among the redwoods and firs
And small mint plants growing out of the rock,
Fragrant with a mysterious, clean smell
That washes the fatigue out of my bones.

I look out at the sun setting beyond the lake.
I listen to raindrops bouncing in the night.
I hear birds waking and welcoming the sun
That casts shadows of mountains
Through our little patch of trees,
And slowly warms the rocks and the air
And the dark water of the lake.

And there is nothing to tell me
That the world is anything
Other than what I see:
Open and interwoven and free.
There is nothing that is out of place,
Nothing that does not belong.
There is nothing that does not welcome Life.

The world is a single place,
And there is a single spirit that blows across its face.

And the name of that Spirit is Life.
Justice, equity, compassion.
Different names for the same thing.

May my senses awaken to the touch of that Spirit.

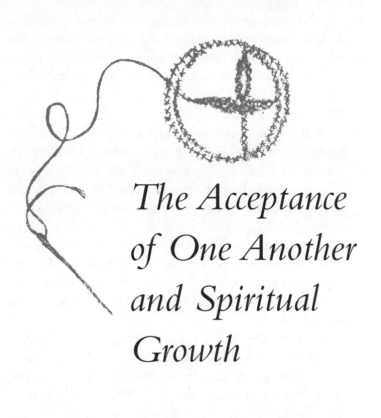

The Acceptance
of One Another
and Spiritual
Growth

Accepting one another sounds like an easy thing. You do your thing, I do mine. As a Hindu friend once told me, you work out your karma, I work out mine, and we all stay out of each other's way. Everybody comes out ahead so long as we don't interfere with each other. What's the big deal?

Well, life is never that straightforward. Suppose my doing my thing makes it hard or even impossible for you to do yours and vice versa. What then? Suppose your understanding of what a church stands for and should be doing is incompatible with my understanding of church. Does one of us have to leave the church? Do we have to work together to create a church that is large enough to support both of us, each simply putting up with the other? Is acceptance nothing more interesting than tolerating other people's eccentricities and peculiar ideas?

If it were that simple I doubt Unitarian Universalists would have felt strongly enough to insist that acceptance appear among our basic Principles. After all, we can put up with a lot of things that we think are silly, ridiculous, muddle-headed, and flat-out wrong. We can put up with people we have no use or respect for. We can even put up with people while showing them little compassion and only the minimum of a grudging sort of justice. If tolerating each other were all there is to acceptance, then acceptance would be so much weaker than the first two Unitarian Universalist Principles that it would not be listed. Acceptance flows out of the belief in the inherent worth and dignity of all. If I truly understand deeply within my heart that the worth and dignity that defines me and makes me human dwells as fully within your heart as it does in mine, then I will not simply put up with you. I will also recognize that my deepening as a human being requires your deepening. Acceptance, in the sense of our Principles, is not of behavior or ideas; it is of people in their basic humanity, their dignity and worth, their needs for companionship, growth, love, compassion, and justice.

Let me illustrate with an example. During the 1960s and 1970s, American culture struggled with what was called the Generation Gap. It was the Baby Boomers versus the Pre-Baby Boomers—now often called the Builders—sometimes with no holds barred. The gap was a deep failure to understand and accept genuine difference, a failure of acceptance. Too many people on both sides of the generational line were more invested in their being right and the other side being wrong than they were in investing in the dignity of each other. They were more interested in being right than in compassion, justice, or acceptance.

Something similar is happening again as my generation of Baby Boomers supplants our parents in positions of leadership in cultural institutions. Consider, for example, the Unitarian Universalist Association. One of the reasons Unitarian Universalist ministers gather periodically is to compare notes about the state of our congregations and to get a sense of what is happening within the movement. Recently many of us around the country have noticed that something potentially disturbing is happening. A growing rift is appearing between people in our congregations, and it is falling out largely, though not exclusively, along generational and, to a lesser extent, gender lines. We are seeing deep differences in such issues as what religion and church are about, what worship is for and how it should be conducted, the use of traditional religious language, the relative importance of feelings and reason in life generally and in religion specifically, and the nature of commitment to an institution, church, or anything else. And as I talk to my colleagues, something I hear over and over is the puzzle that neither side feels that its needs are being met.

The younger generation seems to feel that there is an unspoken orthodoxy that prevents them from articulating and acting on their deepest beliefs and needs, so they feel abandoned, ignored, and even ridiculed. The older generation seems to feel that the church is increasingly deserting them and all they have worked hard for and believed in, and they feel hurt, betrayed, and even ridiculed. More and more of my colleagues report that their younger members are calling for more ritual and a deeper sense of the spiritual in worship, while the older generation is disturbed by the level of ritual we have and wants a return to political and intellectual discussion in worship. In one ear we hear, "Why can't we have prayer?" In the other we hear, "Why can't we have politics?" In one ear we hear, "It's too dry and spiritually empty!" In the other we hear, "There's too much empty ritual and 'symbolism' and not enough intellectual content!"

The first thing to do is to ask the right question. It is tempting to look at this situation and ask who is right. Is the younger generation right in asking for more ritual and spirituality, or is the older generation right in asking for a return to more humanistic values? This is the wrong question. It assumes an all-or-nothing stance, that if one side is right, then the other must be wrong. A more appropriate question is how we can meet both needs in our Unitarian Universalist communities. How can we learn to create religious communities in which we are prepared to invest in both the younger generation's need for spiritual growth and depth and the older generation's need for intellectual depth and content? How can we create religious communities in which people with what appear to be incompatible needs can accept each other, embrace each other's human dignity, and invest in each other's deeper growth and development, even when they do not share belief?

I must admit that I have no answer. I'm not sure that I have asked the question very well or to the satisfaction of either side. The real issue is not of someone being right and therefore someone else being wrong, but the acceptance of one another. It is not just putting up with one another, but investing in each other's inherent worth and dignity. The crisis I see developing in Unitarian Universalism is a spiritual crisis, comparable to the crisis that shook the movement in the first part of the twentieth century when humanism was being born and challenging an entrenched Unitarian Christianity. I see that struggle as a spiritual one that produced enormous spiritual growth in our movement. What we are looking at now can produce the same kind of growth if we allow it.

Sometimes people think that the spiritual is opposed to the mundane or that spirituality is some kind of mystical mumbo-jumbo and nonsense. Neither is the case. If we went back and looked at what the great religious leaders of humanity have taught about spirituality, we would have to conclude that our spiritual lives are not divorced from our day-to-day lives. If they are divorced, we are in very serious trouble.

In the third Unitarian Universalist Principle, the concepts of acceptance and encouragement to spiritual growth are listed together as if they are inextricably intertwined, perhaps different ways of saying the same thing. In our spiritual lives we are who we are, we understand what is required of us, and we accept and embrace the Profound Beauty of our uniqueness in the world. The key is that last phrase: in the world. Our spirituality is living our deepest reality, our deepest truth, our deepest value, into the world. Our spirituality is the unfolding of who we are, and our richest integrity from the deepest places of our hearts into the ordinariness of our living. The first step in this process is accepting ourselves in our own awful beauty and dignity.

This seems to be a lifelong task, not something for Sunday mornings, an occasional weekend workshop, or even a summer institute. It is something we must always do, something we are never finished with, for our lives are constantly unfolding, always a work in progress. Genuine spirituality requires that we be ready to change, to let go of this and embrace that, to be ready when the call comes to return to the journey, the motion, be it outward or inward, be it to adventure or to return home.

I have discovered in my own life that this call to spiritual growth and change is reflected in my ability to extend my acceptance beyond myself. It was and is hard enough to accept the beauty, the inherent value and dignity of myself, but the next step always seems to be moving beyond that, moving outward in acceptance, to enlarge my embrace. What makes that possible is the discovery that my integrity is bound up in the integrity of all. I cannot at the same time embrace myself and reject the world. If I lose the world beyond myself, I will lose myself. If I reject the preciousness of others, I end up rejecting my own preciousness. If I seek to compromise the integrity of any person, then I will in so doing compromise my own.

The church must encourage us to spiritual growth, for where else will we discover a community, a context, and a model for the ability to invest in others so that our own selves become enriched, fulfilled, and new? Where else can we find the support and the understanding that make it possible for us to change, to grow our selves? The great Unitarian minister A. Powell Davies defined religion as the opportunity to grow a soul. A more humanist way of saying the same thing is that religion is the opportunity to become human. How shall we do that if we are trying to prune the soul of another? How shall we do that if we are seeking to stunt the humanity of another? And where shall we grow our souls, become more deeply human, if not in religious community?

How Coyote Lost His Songs, Music, and Dance

Here is a new story about Coyote. One day it occurred to him that he didn't need any of the other creatures. There he was, sitting pretty all by himself. What did he need anyone else for? He had his songs, his flute and drum, and his fire. He had his dancing and his huge tipi. Besides, all the other creatures were kind of strange. There was Rabbit, with his huge ears and enormous legs, and all he ever did was run around. And there was Moose, with that absurd head of antlers, wandering up to his knees in marshes. And there were all these pesky birds, flitting around, twittering, and never letting Coyote nap. Ridiculous! Who needed them? Not Coyote!

So he decided to just leave them all behind. He picked himself up and wandered off, trying to find a place where he could be alone. Entirely alone, with none of these silly and absurd creatures to bother him, where he could dance his dances by himself and sing and play his flute and drum for no one but himself, a place where he wouldn't have to share his fire and he could nap in peace.

As Coyote was leaving, Rabbit happened to see him and tagged along. At first he ran ahead with his big legs and then he ran back, and then ahead, and then back. Coyote ignored him, hoping he would just go away.

"Hey, Coyote," Rabbit yelled. "Where ya goin'?"

Coyote ignored him.

Rabbit ran on ahead and came back. "Hey, Coyote," he said. "Know what's on the other side of that hill? I do. I just saw it."

Coyote was curious, but he ignored Rabbit and just kept on walking. Rabbit ran on ahead and came back.

"Hey, Coyote," he said. "There's something over there, where you're headed, and you ought to know about it. I just saw it. Want me to tell you about it?"

Well, Coyote did want to know, but he just ignored Rabbit, hoping he'd go away and leave him alone. Ridiculous Rabbit.

Rabbit's feeling were a bit hurt. "Coyote, you know what? You're crazy." And he went away.

That night, a funny thing happened. Coyote stopped and built his fire and sat down to sing, as he did every night. But as hard as he tried, he couldn't remember any of his songs. And so all he could do was play his flute and drum, and dance a little. But he couldn't sing. And the night was strangely quiet.

The next day, Coyote was off again, feeling a little sad and a little strange. But he still wanted to get away from these ridiculous creatures with their absurd ways of being. Before long, he came to a marsh. It was so wide he didn't see how he could go around it, and, shrugging his shoulders, he started to go through it.

Pretty soon he ran into Moose, who was as usual up to his knees in mud and weeds. Moose lifted his huge head of antlers when he saw Coyote coming. "Well, hello Coyote," he said. "What brings you way out here to the marshes?"

Coyote ignored him and kept looking for a way to cross the mud. Moose swung his great head this way and that, a little miffed that Coyote was ignoring him.

"Coyote, if you're looking for a dry path, I could help you," he said.

Coyote looked right at him and said nothing. What a ridiculous creature, Coyote thought to himself. If I had such silly things growing out of my head, I wouldn't let anyone see them!

Moose's feelings really were hurt by now. "You know what, Coyote? You're crazy!" And Moose walked away.

Coyote finally did find his way across the marsh and went on. That night something strange happened. Again, Coyote built his fire and tried to make his music, but not only had he forgotten his songs, now he couldn't remember how to play his flute and drum. All he could do was dance around the fire. And the night was frighteningly silent.

The next day, Coyote was really upset and a little afraid, but he had decided that he would get away from all these silly creatures and get away he would. So he set off again. This time, he came to a little stream that flowed down out of the mountains. All along its banks were bushes and flowers and it was beautiful and still and cool. And since he was thirsty and a little tired,

Coyote took a long drink, sat down, and decided to take a nap.

As they often are, the bushes were filled with birds, and just as Coyote was about to go to sleep, the little birds started singing their songs. This was exactly what he wanted to get away from. It really made him angry that the birds wouldn't let him sleep in peace. And he was a little afraid and jealous that they could sing and he had forgotten his songs and even how to sing. And so he leaped up and snarled and barked at them to frighten them away.

And he succeeded. They flew up and off. But one bird, a little braver than the others, said to him—being careful to fly just out of his reach—"Coyote, you're crazy!" And off she went.

Coyote was kind of pleased with himself for getting rid of the birds and so he decided to stay right there. That night he made his fire, but the strangest thing happened. Not only could he no longer sing, and not only could he no longer play his flute and drum, but now he couldn't even remember how to dance! All Coyote could do was stare into the silent fire and think about how much he had lost.

Finally he fell asleep and dreamed. In his dream, White Buffalo Woman appeared to him and asked him why he was so sad and scared. Coyote explained how he had lost his songs and music and dance. He didn't know what to do, and he was afraid that he would also lose his fire.

White Buffalo Woman asked him why he was out here all alone. Coyote explained that he was tired of being surrounded all the time by those silly creatures who looked strange and acted strange and lived such ridiculous lives, and he had decided that he would live by himself, away from them all.

"Coyote," said White Buffalo Woman, "don't you understand that your music and your dance, and even your fire, are nothing but the spirits of those creatures who are different from you? As you drove them away, they left even your heart and took their spirits with them. If you want your music and dance back, you must go back to your friends and accept them back into your heart. Only then will you be able to go on."

The next morning when Coyote awoke, he couldn't remember his dream, but when the birds began to sing, as they always do in the morning, he sat still and listened to them. And then he began to go back the way he had come. That night when he built his fire, he could remember his dance. And the next day he went off, back the way he had come, and chanced upon Moose. And he asked Moose how to get across the marsh. That night, when he built his fire, he remembered how to play his flute and drum and the night was not so lonely. And the next day he still went back the way he had come, and suddenly up ran Rabbit. Coyote ran with Rabbit and played and had a good old time. And that night, when he had built his fire, the air was filled with Coyote's songs. And never again did Coyote forget how easily he could lose his music and his dance and even his fire.

The Dance of Time

Does the rose envy the sunset for its orange
Or the sea envy the lake for its calm?
Does the sky blame the earth for being brown
Or the whale blame the fish for laying eggs?

Does the redwood disregard the sorrel for being small
Or the desert think less of the marsh for being wet?
Does the bird laugh at the snail that cannot fly
Or the otter tease the rock that meditates in the river?

Are the stars embarrassed at the brightness of the moon,
Or is the rain afraid of the cold of the snow?
Does the pine turn its head from the nakedness
     of the oak
Or the corn, row on row, from the wild grass?

     And am I less than the trees and stars and rose
     That I should turn my face from the soul of another?

And the dance of time goes on without stop or pause.
The dance goes on. Day after turning day,
Night after spinning night on it goes and on and on.
Leaping minutes, pirouette, grand jeté,
Plié, turn and spin and lift and leap,
On and on without end or pause.

Silent music rising out of the heart,

Turning the hours, moving the dancers
Each to a private music unheard by others,
Each turning and spinning alone yet joined
To the others by invisible threads of dance that weave
A pattern of exquisite, profound beauty.

And all of this happens around me at every moment,
As the hours move, turn, and spin through my life.

*A Free and
Responsible
Search for Truth
and Meaning*

As a former teacher of philosophy, I ask myself whether our Unitarian Universalist Principles are really about the theory of knowledge. Do our Principles spring from philosophy or religion? To be sure, religion and philosophy are intimately tied to each other. After all, in the Scholastic view of philosophy, theology was one of the major branches of metaphysics.

But I took part in the debate over the adoption of our Principles in the early 1980s, and I do not recall hearing other Unitarian Universalists raise any distinctly philosophical questions. They were utterly beside the point, even though one could—and in the proper context one should—raise them and ask what a Unitarian Universalist philosophy would be. Instead, what I remember is people asking religious questions, wondering what it is that changes people's lives. I remember people wanting a statement of Unitarian Universalist principles that would allow us to examine our own lives and discover depth and subtlety and strength and love and worth.

In trying to understand our fourth Unitarian Universalist Principle—a free and responsible search for truth and meaning—I must ask the following questions: What is truth, not in the sense of science or philosophy, but in the sense of religion? Where does meaning lie? How can we find truth and meaning within our own lives? What makes our own search for truth and meaning responsible—and disciplined? What is the truth that heals a broken life? I hesitate to ask what is the meaning of life because it is a cliché, but that, too, is one of the questions that needs to be raised. And these questions raise further difficult questions about the relativity or universality of meaning. In fact, these questions threaten to take us right back into philosophy, to the epistemology of religion.

Trying to answer these questions in any detail is more than I can address in this essay. But it is interesting to see how extensive, substantive, and rich our Principles are. The questions I ask can only scratch the surface in interpreting our Principles. For now I would like to explore a small segment of what I take to be the lived part of this iceberg called truth and meaning.

I wrote the following story, "The Hidden Treasure of Lvov," as an example of the search for religious or spiritual truth and meaning, although it is couched in terms of a search for treasure. If you are acquainted with Joseph Campbell's classic study *The Hero With a Thousand Faces,* you will recognize that my character, the Rabbi of Lvov, is on a hero's journey. The Rabbi is called by his dream. He goes off, although reluctantly, in search of a boon. He encounters difficulty and loss on the way and receives help from an unexpected and unanticipated source. He receives his boon and returns to share it with his people. The Rabbi's journey is what I think the fourth Principle is about. In our lives we are being called to find our treasure, our boon, to discover the hero within our own hearts.

I am well aware of the feminist critique of most analyses of the hero's journey, including Campbell's. Most stories of this type are cast in terms of a journey outward and seem to ignore the journey inward. Most of the heroes are men who engage in male adventure, often involving killing and battle and war. They move forward in an episodic way, from one major crisis to another. The reward is often wealth or power or the king's daughter. These criticisms are all true, but they are merely critiques of the surface, not of the substance of the hero's journey.

Let me outline the idea in somewhat different though still metaphorical terms. We are assured in the first Principle that each one of us carries in our own lives a jewel of great worth and dignity. This jewel shines with the light of a thousand stars, yet it is so well hidden within us that we must discover it. As we grow into adulthood, at some point we encounter this jewel for the first time, this worth and dignity, within our hearts and souls. And when that happens, our lives are changed. We are called to make this jewel visible in the living of our lives. We are called to become something that we have not been. And we are called to follow ever more deeply and honestly the light of that treasure.

This journey doesn't have anything to do with being male or female, humanist or theist, Christian, Buddhist, Pagan, or Hindu. It doesn't have anything to do with the specifics, the surface of life, except as the surface carries the imprint of the depth. It has to do with being and becoming human. A theist might articulate the call to her journey in terms of an encounter with God and the journey itself in terms of following God's will. A humanist might articulate it in terms of encountering the profound reality of human depth and the cultivation and full flowering of his humanity. In spite of appearances, I think that they are both talking about the same thing, their own journey as a hero, but using different terms to describe their experience.

People often tell me that they have great difficulty seeing their own lives as a hero's journey. They cannot see that they were called to anything. They cannot see that they have discovered any treasure hidden under the floor, any Golden Fleece, or any great and miraculous insight to share with the world. They see nothing spectacular about their lives, only a slow unfolding of life, now painful, now filled with happiness. Where's the hero? Where's the journey? Where's the boon? Where's the treasure?

The Rabbi of Lvov found his treasure under the floor of his own home. He had traveled all the way to Vienna only to be told that he had to go home again to find the treasure. He had to discover that the treasure lay under the floorboards of his own ordinary life. And that is how it is with us.

The treasure, the hero's boon, the worth, the dignity, the Profound Beauty, cannot be found out there, in some far, exotic place. It can be found only within the human heart, within the souls of our lives, under the floorboards of our living. It is not something that someone else can give you; it is something that you have to discover for yourself. It is not something that you have to search through ancient and dusty tomes to find. It is something that is as near as the floorboards of your own home, your own heart, mind, and soul. It is not something that is different from you or your life. It is you. It is your worth and dignity, your integrity, your humanity, your sacred reality. And it is your task as a human being to find it and make it real in the living of your life. This is the religious and spiritual task of life: the realization, the making real, of the Profound Beauty, the Untarnishable Integrity that defines you.

Among other things, this means that the hero's journey is ultimately autobiographical and never prescriptive to anyone but the hero—and we're all heroes in our own lives. Whatever I may discover under my floorboards is something I need to give myself to, but I cannot impose it on anyone else. It cannot be the end of any journey but my own. The Rabbi of Lvov offered his treasure to his community so that it could build a synagogue and school. He did not try to impose his treasure on others, but instead he offered his treasure as a way to help others to discover their own. And that is all that anyone can do. Ralph Waldo Emerson told the graduates of Harvard Divinity School that they must offer congregations their lives "passed through the fire of thought," not to impose their insight on their parishioners, but to illuminate for their congregations the discovery of their own insight, integrity, Profound Beauty, truth, and meaning.

The fourth Principle talks about a search for truth and meaning. It is therefore also about how Unitarian Universalism is a spiritual path. When I talk about spirituality, I am not talking about something hidden and dark, forbidding and grim, even meaningless. To be religious, to live a genuinely spiritual life, is to embrace a tradition and a history and to make it your own. When a Jewish child comes of age, he or she becomes *Bar* (or *Bat*) *Mitzvah*, which means "Child of the Law." At that point, children become adults because they embrace the Jewish law and tradition and make them their own. They commit themselves to following the journey into Jewish truth and life. With all religious traditions or practices, to be spiritual is to follow the journey into truth and meaning, to discover the treasure and to make it real and visible in the living of our lives.

However your life unfolds, that is your journey. And you are the hero of that journey. The first Principle tells us that there is worth and dignity, Profound Beauty, treasure under the floorboards of every human life. And the fourth Principle tells us that we can find it if we search diligently, responsibly, thoroughly, and freely, and that we can make it real in the living of our lives, day by day by day. This Principle moves from the promise of worth into the living of life, and so it is here that we discover ours is both a religion and a spiritual path.

The Hidden Treasure of Lvov

There was once a rabbi named Schmuel who was, although pious, reverent, and kind, very poor. He lived alone in a small village in the Ukraine, near the town of Lvov. His house was small and since he could only afford the bare essentials of life, he depended on the generosity of others to pay his taxes. But since Schmuel was a good, wise, and gentle man, everyone in the Jewish community loved him. Even the Gentiles held him in high respect, and if sometimes he didn't have quite enough, they would forgive his debts.

One night Schmuel went to sleep and dreamed of a bridge in Vienna. In his dream he saw the bridge and someone burying a treasure at a certain spot under it. Then he heard a voice telling him that if he could find the treasure, it would be his. When Schmuel awoke, he was troubled. After all, he said to himself, the treasure was someone else's, not his. Someone else had hidden it, and so even if he did find it, it would not be his. So he went to confer with some other rabbis, and they all told him that since he was told in the dream that the treasure would be his when he found it, he should go to Vienna and dig it up. Schmuel still wasn't sure, but he followed their advice and started out for Vienna.

It is a long way from Lvov to Vienna and Schmuel

couldn't afford so much as a horse, let alone coach fare. He had to walk the whole way, often sleeping in a haystack or barn and begging for food. But eventually he arrived and went straight to the bridge to find the treasure. When he got to the bridge, he discovered that the emperor's army had placed a guard there. Well, Schmuel couldn't go around digging up the land under the bridge right under the nose of one of the emperor's guards! So he decided to wait for his opportunity.

Every day Schmuel came out to the bridge and just wandered back and forth over it, waiting to see when he could go and dig up the treasure. After a few days, the guard noticed this shabby old rabbi going back and forth over the bridge and hanging around as if waiting. After a few days more, the guard came over to him.

"Rabbi," he said. "I see you every day, walking back and forth across the bridge. Is there something I can do for you? Are you waiting for someone or something?"

"Yes," said Schmuel. "I have come all the way from the Ukraine on foot because in a dream I saw a treasure here in Vienna."

At this the guard laughed out loud. "Meaning no disrespect, Rabbi, but surely you can't be serious. Coming all the way from Lvov because of a dream! Why, if I took dreams seriously, I myself would have resigned from the army long ago. When I was about twenty years old, I had a dream in which I saw a treasure buried under the floor of a hut in Lvov that belonged to a poor Jew named

Schmuel. When I woke up I first wanted to go find the treasure, but then, when I thought more about it, I realized how ridiculous it all was. Can you imagine! Lvov, where half the people are Jews named Schmuel! My advice to you is to go back to your people and forget all about this dream."

Schmuel thanked the guard for his advice and immediately went back to Lvov. When he finally arrived, he was even more tired, disheveled, and worn than ever, but he went to work immediately digging up the floor of his hut. And in only a little time, he discovered the treasure, hidden there for who knows how long.

And do you know what Schmuel did with his treasure? He kept a little for himself, true, but most of it he gave away to his people. With his money they built a grand synagogue, large enough for the whole community to come and worship, and with what was left over, they built a school so that the children would learn to read and study the Torah.

It Is Always There

And sometimes it is as obvious as a rock:
Solid, unmistakable, sparkling in the sunlight.
Sometimes it stands up and almost shouts at me
Like lightning splitting the summer air,
Like water stumbling down a thousand feet
And exploding against the earth in shimmering drops
That hang for a moment in the sun and fall again
Into a white swirling pool of darkness
That gathers and flows outward into the river.
Sometimes it is as obvious as life.

And sometimes it is as shy as a butterfly
Hiding in the flowers, dancing in the sun
In and out of the edges of sight,
Now here, now invisible as air.
Sometimes it is no more than a suggestion,
A promise, a tease, hardly enough to believe in,
Darting behind a curtain, hidden as the sky
When the fog descends, carefully, silently,
Like a doe crossing an open field.
Sometimes it is as hidden as fawn.

And sometimes it is as excruciating
As a fingernail drawn across a wall,
As painful as falling naked into a bed of nettles.

Sometimes it seems to have been stolen,
Eaten right out of my heart,
Eaten like rats gnawing their way
Into the granary and helping themselves,
Stealing the pristine wheat. Sometimes
It is as excruciating as death and madness.

And it is always there, like love is there.
Whether it fairly shouts at me or hides,
Whether it turns and turns in my heart
Like a slowly turning dagger, it is there.
And I shall find it.

*The Right
of Conscience
and the
Use of the
Democratic
Process*

People unfamiliar with Unitarian Universalism may wonder why we have enshrined the democratic process and the right of conscience among our basic Principles. How is democracy a religious issue? What has the right of conscience to do with how a community is ruled? What has the democratic spirit to do with us as a religious community?

Democracy is the rule of and for the people, and one way of allowing people to rule themselves is to allow the majority to govern most of the time. One may reason that democracy is nothing more than a way of organizing ourselves for the smooth functioning of the community. If people can agree to allow a majority to control the group, more often than not the community will be well governed. But what does that have to do with religion and with conscience?

There is more to democracy than a simple counting of noses. Our terrible history of slavery and racism illustrates better than almost anything how terribly wrong the majority can be and how much pain a tyranny of the majority can create. Furthermore, it should never be forgotten that not only can the majority be terribly wrong, but the majority is not the people. It is only the largest fraction of the people. (And occasionally in this "democracy" of ours it is not even that. When a significant enough portion of the electorate do not vote, then even a very small fraction of the people can determine the outcome of an election.)

The idea of self-rule is based on a religious idea: people should rule themselves because no one is privileged. That no one is privileged follows from something that we Unitarian Universalists take as a given, namely that every person contains inherent worth and dignity. If each person is equally worthy, then no one is more worthy than others. Because no one is privileged, it follows that each person in the community is responsible for the well-being of every other person and all are equally responsible. But if all are responsible, then all should participate in governing, and democracy is the best way we know to accomplish this.

The right of conscience also flows as obviously from the first Principle as water flows from a pitcher. Consider what the right of conscience is. Is it not our very worth and dignity becoming manifest in people's minds? My conscience is not simply a matter of conditioned response to stimulus. It is far deeper; it is the way my being, my very self, responds to the world around me. If I am repulsed by some things and moved by others, that tells me how I am connected with all. It tells me how I must promote the well-being of all. It tells me that I am responsible for all and how to exercise that responsibility while retaining the humility to recognize that, even when most people agree with me, I may be wrong. I may be reading the "still, small voice" of conscience incorrectly.

I use the phrase "still, small voice" on purpose. It

comes from the Bible, from an incident in the story of the prophet Elijah. When King Ahab decreed that Elijah should be put to death, he fled to the mountains to escape. There in a cave he prayed to God, saying that he had had enough and wanted God to take his life. An angel told Elijah to come to the mouth of the cave so that he might stand before God. Elijah did so, and there came an enormous wind, so strong that it uprooted trees and blew the rocks about, but God was not in the wind. And the wind was followed by an earthquake that opened the earth and threw down hills. But God was not in the earthquake. And the earthquake was followed by fire that fell from the heavens and burned what the wind and earthquake had not destroyed. But God was not in the fire—because God is not destructive.

All of this destructive force was followed by a still, small voice that Elijah heard within his soul, and God was in the still, small voice. The voice told him to take heart and to go back the way he had come. As far as I have found, this is the first time in the literature of the people of ancient Israel that God is found within the heart instead of externally. Usually God speaks from the top of a mountain, or from heaven, speaking as something different from us. Here for the first time God speaks to the prophet from within his own heart, as the most intimate part of himself. It is the voice of conscience.

There are many people for whom the mythic language of this story—couched in terms of the God of

Israel—is at best silent and at worst off-putting. But whatever mythic language may move you, I invite you to think about this story and what it says about conscience. Conscience is not the voice of conventional morality. It is the voice that pulls us deeper and more directly into the worth of all. If you speak the mythic language of theism, it is the voice of the immanent God speaking within your soul. If you speak the mythic language of humanism, it is the voice of the Profound Human Spirit as it lives within you.

Conscience is a manifestation of what Taoists call *Te*, the movement of the unnamable *Tao* that gives each of us our individual strength and power. It is the voice of what Plato referred to as *areté*, the wisdom or virtue of your soul that makes you the unique and precious person you are. It is the upwelling of that which the Buddhists call the Buddha-nature that permits every person—and even every sentient being—to achieve enlightenment. To the Hindu it is the image of that special step in Shiva's dance that brings you into existence and allows you to be. It is that which impels us to the Good, that which ennobles and elevates and frees and heals. It is that which must be stifled and ignored when we do injury and harm and bring brokenness to life. Conscience is central in every tradition. Unitarian Universalists think of it as the manifestation of our inherent worth and dignity. Every tradition calls on its adherents to make conscience visible, real, and manifest

75

in their living. This is the call of conscience, and there could not be religion without it.

How can there be a democratic spirit without this sense of conscience? Unitarian Universalists believe in the democratic method, not because it is the most practical form of government—which it often isn't—or because we think that somehow the will of the majority is magically right—which is manifestly not the case. We believe in the democratic spirit because we believe in the right and exercise of conscience. We believe in the democratic spirit because we believe that there is no other way to safeguard the right of conscience and its unfettered exercise. We believe in the democratic spirit because we believe that privilege, inequality, and oppressive hierarchy are immoral, irreligious, and, if you will, sinful. It is hypocritical to uphold the inherent worth and dignity of all and the right of conscience while supporting privilege and the suppression of any minority, whether racial, sexual, or any other minority.

I am afraid that America is in danger of losing sight of this. Unitarian Universalists fall along all points of the political spectrum, so I am reluctant to make political judgments. But what I am about to say has nothing to do with being liberal or conservative, Democrat or Republican. It has to do with the democratic spirit, with the core of democracy.

Think about the 1994 election. I can't count how many commentators I have read and heard trying to discover what the electorate was saying in this election. There was far more said in the silence of those who did not vote than in the noise of those who did. And the central message was that most Americans believe that far too many of our political leaders have forgotten the democratic spirit, the spirit of respect for difference and diversity, of compassion and communal help. Far too many of our political leaders have forgotten that each is responsible for all and that democracy is first and foremost a safe guard to conscience. I noticed this almost thirty years go when it dawned on me how terribly wrong things had gone when the slogan "Power to the people" had become a radical slogan. Shouldn't that be the motto of a democracy? I can't see that things have changed much in thirty years. It's still a radical notion.

Consider one example, the speech that House Speaker Newt Gingrich gave to the 1995 Republican Annual Convention. I do not want to anger anyone who is a Republican or believes in and supports Speaker Gingrich. But he said something in that speech that I found very disturbing. He attacked the Democratic party, which is to be expected. He said the Democrats would do anything to maintain power: lie, cheat, break if not the letter then the spirit of the law, and be ruthless obstructionists. Newt Gingrich would therefore oppose them every step of the way, with every weapon at his command.

This is something that I find frightening, not because I disagree with Gingrich's conservative program, but because it is the stuff of disrespect and demagoguery. He shows no respect for people who disagree with him and no humility in his thought. It was as if he were saying that if you disagree with him, you are not only wrong, you are a force that needs maximum opposition, for if you succeed, you will bring the country down. This is hubris at its worst. There is nothing more dangerous to the democratic spirit and the right of conscience than hubris. (The word "hubris," incidentally, comes from a Greek word that means "violence.")

Democracy requires as much cooperation and acceptance of diversity as does religion. In John Locke's "Letter Concerning Toleration" (which was written about toleration in religion but I have paraphrased in some places to discuss government) he wrote:

It is not the diversity of opinions, (which cannot be avoided) but the refusal of toleration to those that are of different opinions, (which might have been granted) that has produced all the bustles and wars, that have been in the . . . world, upon account of [government]. The heads and leaders of the [State], moved by avarice and insatiable desire for dominion, making use of the immoderate ambition of magistrates, and the credulous superstition of the giddy multitude have incensed and animated them against those that dissent from themselves; by preaching unto them, contrary to the laws of . . . [democracy], and the precepts of charity, that [dissidents and opponents] are to be outed of their possessions, and destroyed.

However unwittingly, we are in danger of handing our democracy over to those who will, perhaps even in the name of its preservation, destroy it.

This same anti-democratic spirit is exhibited in a people who would rather build prisons than schools and who would rather punish crime than prevent it. It is exhibited when it is impossible to get people to pass bond issues and tax measures that would allow schools to employ creative, excited teachers, and to be safe and exciting places for children to learn. It is exhibited when we punish children for the sins of their parents or deny children the opportunity to rise above the poverty into which they were born.

The fifth Unitarian Universalist Principle is important. Perhaps it is more important now, at this point in American history, than at any time since the US Civil War, and it explains why it is important that Unitarian Universalism grow and spread its message. It is not simply so that there will be more Unitarian Universalists, but because we bear a responsibility to bring this Principle, which is part of the core of our teachings, to life. This is the principle that incarnates in culture and government our dedication to the inherent worth and dignity of all. This is the principle that brings us face to face with the necessity of compassion and love, not as mere intellectual, philosophical principles, but as something real and in the flesh, for that is the dress that the democratic spirit must wear. Our movement must spread and grow because America needs this principle. If we, for whom it is central, do not live within its spirit and work hard for its manifestation, who will? And if not now, when?

Shirley's Story

When I was a child, blacks and the whites went to separate schools. Most people thought that the races should have very little to do with each other. I can remember that there were separate restrooms for whites and blacks, separate restaurants, separate sections of movie theaters, and so on. But as a child, I didn't think much about it. It was just the way things were. It didn't occur to me that this sort of thing hurt people.

When I was nine years old, the decision was made that we would no longer have separate schools for blacks and whites in this country. It was not a popular decision. Many people thought that it was awful and that it would only lead to trouble. The school I was attending was a small, country school. It had six grades but only four classrooms. Just before I started fifth grade, the decision was made that ours would be one of the schools that would be "integrated," which meant that there would be black students. Actually there was only one at first, a black girl named Shirley in the sixth grade.

At first nothing much happened. School was school, after all, and she was only one more kid in my class, which was a mixed class of fifth and sixth grades. Most kids paid little attention to all of the fuss. But somehow the idea seeped into us that there was something odd, something peculiar and maybe even a little dangerous about Shirley being in our class. Maybe it was just the kind of listening to adults that children do. We began to get the idea that Shirley did not belong with us.

At first Shirley's mother had to drive her to school because the school bus wouldn't stop for her. But driving her daughter to school every day and picking her up got old, especially when almost every other student in the school rode on the bus. Finally Shirley's mother went to court to force the school to provide bus transportation for Shirley. A little bit later everything boiled over.

I came out to recess one day a little later than usual and I heard a huge commotion on one side of the schoolyard. There were lots of students calling and singing and standing in a circle around something, so I went over to see what was going on. And there were about fifty kids surrounding Shirley in a circle, taunting her and chanting racial insults at her. And there was nothing she could do. She was crying and angry and hurt and humiliated and helpless. I saw the look of terror and pain in her eyes, and for the first time I realized that racism hurts human beings.

I wish I could say that I did something about it, but I didn't. I didn't take part in it, but I also did nothing to stop it. I didn't even go to find a teacher. I just stood there. And to this day I am ashamed of myself that I didn't even try to find an adult to intervene. I just stood there and watched this terrible thing happening to Shirley.

Racism is not just something that adults talk about. It is also something that gets inside of people and makes them do terrible things to each other. It makes people hurt each other and hate each other and then laugh at the pain. It is a terrible, terrible thing, and it is a thing that is real. We must all become aware of each other and the pain that we can cause. The adult way of saying this is that we must be compassionate with each other, that we must learn how to comfort the pain in each other's lives. Perhaps if we all can do this, if we all can become more compassionate with each other, then the day will come that racism will live only in our history books and not in the lives of our people.

The Center of the Universe

Where is the center of the universe?

Is it over there, near the sun?
Is it perhaps off in the stars,
Hidden in the center of the galaxy,
Surrounded by light and energy
And the enormous heat generated by billions of stars?
Or is it somewhere hidden in the middle of nowhere
Away and away from everything else,
Surrounded by nothing more than nothing?

Or maybe it is nearer,
Beside this oak growing alone
On top of a thousand-foot cliff,
Overlooking the sea. And maybe
The osprey that rests in the tree
Overlooking the ocean sits
Right in the center of the universe,
And looks out, not at the sea, but at everything.

But no. It is nearer.
Maybe the center of the universe lies
Right inside my own heart.
Maybe it is I who look out at everything.
Maybe the osprey and the oak and even the stars
Circle and circle and seek so desperately

For the gem that lies hidden in my own heart,
Hidden and alone, and I hold the secret.

But no. It is even nearer yet.
The center of the universe is so near
That I cannot ever find it,
So near that it cannot even be lost.
The center of the universe is so near that
Wherever I look, wherever I turn my head
And search, there it is,
                there it is,
                there it is.

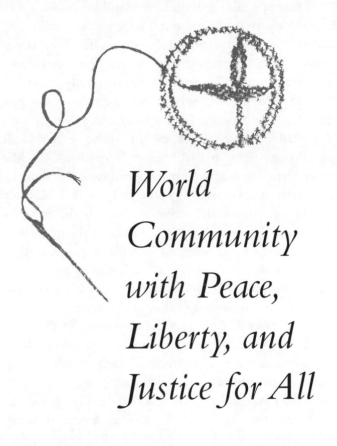

*World
Community
with Peace,
Liberty, and
Justice for All*

For some people the sixth Unitarian Universalist Principle has an odd ring to it. I have a friend who calls this the "Superman Principle" and says that every time he hears it, he expects it to end with the words "and the American way." There is something terribly "sixties" about that. Many of us who grew up in the sixties just assumed that everything labeled American was automatically terrible, oppressive, unjust, and to be resisted at all costs. Many of us spelled "America" with a "k." My friend's remark smacks of that mentality, and I want to say that it is dead wrong. Not only is it a blunder to think of "American" as synonymous with "conventional" and "bourgeois" or "evil," but this principle stands at the center of our religious and other communities. It is crucial to our existence as a religious movement.

Let us begin with the idea of community. Unitarian Universalists sometimes spend so much time and energy worrying about and praising the autonomy of the individual that we forget that individuals standing alone have about as much strength as a bunch of stones lying around on the ground. It is only when a mason picks up these stones and builds a wall that they become powerful. And that is how it is with communities. Alone, we're not much; together we have power. In fact, some people believe that the idea of an individual makes no sense except in the context of a community. Could you have a wife or a husband and no marriage? How can you have individuals who have no relationships or communal ties?

88

Let us look carefully at this idea of community using the Chinese diagram of Yin and Yang. This diagram has symmetry to it, but it is not the static symmetry of a mirror that we in the West like so much. It is a dynamic, circular symmetry. Think of Yin and Yang as two fish in constant motion, swimming together, chasing each other, one constantly moving in to replace the other, on and on in a circle forever. There is tension between them, but it is not a destructive one. It is a dynamic, creative, ongoing, and powerful tension. It is the kind of tension created in music between contrasting keys and in painting between colors and in dance between moving bodies. In classical China, the Yin and Yang diagram was named "the Supreme Ultimate," not for the Yin and Yang, but for the circle their tension creates. This is what community is about, the kind of dynamic, creative tension that requires people to move together in a sort of dance. You can't have a community of one, just as you can't have Yin without Yang. You can't have full, deep, and healed humanity in isolation.

This reminds me of a favorite story told to me by the Reverend William Schulz. In the Middle Ages, a certain order of monks lived quietly at their monastery and part of their rule was that periodically they each go on an individual retreat. The length of the retreat was up to the individual monk and for some it would last a very long time indeed. One day a monk sought out the Abbot and asked for permission to go on his retreat. The

Abbot gave his permission and off the monk went.

The monk came to the hermitage and opened a Bible that was there. It happened to open to a passage in the Gospel of John that described Jesus washing his disciples' feet. The monk read that passage and meditated on it for a couple of days, then abruptly got up and returned to the monastery. As was the custom, he presented himself to the Abbot, who was surprised to see him return so soon.

"So. You have returned already," said the Abbot.

The monk replied, "Of course. For whose feet would the hermit wash?"

And that is what community is about. It is about washing feet, serving each other in humility and generosity. It is about creating ways to help each other. It is what Rabbi Moshe Lieb of Sassov meant when he said that there is always a way to help. And if there isn't, invent one. It is about reaching to each other and touching, sometimes literally, with a gentle and healing hand, sometimes with food or clothing, sometimes with a place of shelter, sometimes with a mind or a heart, sometimes with the caress of a soul. And it means reaching out and asking for help, for do we not deny each other when we refuse to give to others the opportunity to help us?

In the first Unitarian Universalist Principle, we extol the inherent worth and dignity of each human being. Yet it remains true that with no one's feet to wash, it is impossible for that very worth and dignity to be manifest or celebrated. In community it becomes possible for our humanity to grow, flower, and bear fruit. We never come to fruition alone and in a vacuum, but only in community, touching and serving each other, and living in creative tension together.

It is right to compare a community to a marriage, because it is in our familial relationships that we learn to cherish connection, and connection is the soul of community. Isn't the love of someone the primal community? We keep hearing and reading about the demise of marriage and the family. I say that all of this is pure hogwash. We have allowed the demagogues of the political and religious right and the shallow and misguided to steal from us one of our most cherished values, the value of family and community.

It may well happen that the structure of marriage and family will change, but that is nothing new. Like everything human, everything living, the idea of family must change and grow. But the idea of coming together with people you love and forming a communal unit in which you can become ever more deeply human, and ever more deeply real in your own dignity, a unit in which the dynamic tension between you and another loved human being creates a healing context in which the Profound Beauty of both your lives becomes real as you move together, one's Yin to the other's Yang, that idea is fundamental to human living, fundamental to peace, liberty, and justice. And I will never allow any fool of a politician or demagogic preacher to steal that value from me or to force it into a preconceived and stifling mold.

The demagogues are right to link community to family, but they would kill the family and then the community by forcing them to remain, not stable, but stagnant. You cannot preserve a living thing by holding it in stasis. The core of a family is also the core of a community, and that core is love, the profound understanding of connection and the possibility of transformation within a nurturing and supportive context. And if that core of love, support, and nurture are present, who is anyone to say that it is not a family or a community, no matter what its shape, structure, or basis?

It is a perversion of the notion of family values to use the idea of a family and a community to divide, separate, and persecute people. How is it possible to achieve a measure of peace when we use our power not to heal but to harm, not to build but to destroy, not to bring people together but to drive people apart? How is it possible to bring liberty to people when we deny them the right to live as they will and take from them the opportunity to freely become the precious and holy human beings they are? How is it possible to achieve justice when, in the name of love, we deny love?

Plato said that the primary sense of justice is a harmony within the soul and that the idea of political justice derives from that. Black Elk admonished us to be as relatives to all beings, and he said that there can be no peace between people or nations unless there is peace within the soul. According to the etymology of the word, "liberty" is the freedom to grow, to which I would add that it is the freedom to grow into a deeper, richer, fuller, more complete human being. If all this is right, then at the deepest and most fundamental level, peace, liberty, and justice are synonyms, and each requires a community of people who understand connection, touch, dynamic tension, and the washing of feet.

In the Gospel of Luke, Jesus said that to love God as deeply as the Torah requires, we must love our neighbors as ourselves. He was immediately challenged and asked who our neighbors are. His response was the story of the Good Samaritan. I have given the Unitarian Universalist version of his answer in my story "Yammani and the Soji." To realize the Profound Beauty of who we genuinely are, we must stand, not alone, but in deep and loving familial and communal relationships. We must wash our neighbors' feet. But who are our neighbors? With whom must we build a community? Whom must we love? Let me use a metaphor.

A pebble falls into a pond. A little splash and rivulets of waves spread outward in circles. The circles spread all the way across the surface of the pond. Deep beneath the surface, the water remains clear, cool, and still, but circle after circle of little waves spread on the surface. You are the pebble. Life is the pond. Your love is the rivulets of waves. Let your love spread across the whole surface of life, for the water, the life and dignity of all, is the same.

And so we reach out where and as we are able. And we love as we are able. If we live within that creative, dynamic tension, constantly finding new ways and new places to extend our love and to accept the challenge of the acceptance of love, it is enough, it is good.

Water flows and fills the tiniest crevices without judgment. It brings life equally to nematodes, slime molds, roses, great whales, and human beings. There is no judgment; it simply brings the world to life. So may it be with our love; so may it be with our families; so may it be with our communities. And may we find peace, liberty, and justice filling the days of our lives and spreading outward, touching the lives of all, that we may all grow ever more deeply, ever more fully, ever more genuinely human, connected, healed, and at peace. And may we be as relatives to all beings.

Hare's Gifts

This is a story about Hare. Back in the old days, no one lived in towns or villages. Instead, everyone just set up a hut any old place. It was a trifle inconvenient, but it never occurred to anyone to live in any other way.

One day Hyena decided to set up a new hut that would be the biggest and grandest ever made. He searched out a good site near sweet water and in the cool shade of an enormous baobob tree and set out to build the hut. In time it was finished, and it was indeed grand. It was enormously tall and its walls were white and bright and decorated with the most wonderful designs: zigzags and spirals and circles.

Hyena was proud of his new hut and decided to have a feast to show it off. He went around to all of the other huts and invited everyone—even Hare. And everyone came and admired Hyena's hut and then stayed to have a good time—that is, everyone except Hare, who didn't bother to come at all.

The next day Hyena, who was insulted by Hare's not coming to the feast, went to him and grabbed him angrily and demanded to know why he hadn't come to admire the grand new hut.

"Grand new hut! Bah!" snorted Hare. "Why should I come to see your hut? I could build a better one in half the time. And as for your feast, why should I come to your feast and be bored? I could give a feast that would make everyone forget yours."

Hyena stepped back and with a smug smile, said, "All right. It took me a full moon to build and decorate my hut. You have half a moon. And your feast had better be a good one. As for me, I expect that my winter robe will be made of Hare skin."

Hyena left. Hare scratched his head and said to himself, "You've really done it this time, Hare. When will you learn to keep your big mouth shut?" And he sat down to think about what on earth he was going to do. Suddenly he had an idea and jumped up and ran to all of the other huts scattered across the land to ask everyone to come and help him. To get them to come, he promised everyone two marvelous, unheard-of gifts and a wonderful feast when all the work was finished.

The people came in, one family at a time, and Hare showed them where to set up their huts. When everyone had arrived, they set to work. The best workers on wood found, straightened, and set the poles; the best painters mixed and painted the walls; the best artists set to decorating them; and all the others began to prepare the food and drink for the feast.

In short, Hare managed to get everyone else to do all the work. While everyone else was working, he searched around and found a hollow log and a couple of sticks. And then he spent the entire half moon fiddling around with his log and sticks.

At the end of the half moon, Hyena came back, smiling and sharpening his skinning knife. Hare showed him the new hut. There is was, looking very much like Hyena's.

"And just how is this better than my hut?" demanded Hyena, smiling even more and testing the blade of his knife.

"What are you, blind as well as stupid? Just look around, and you'll see," said Hare.

And there arrayed around Hare's hut were the huts of all the people, arranged in a circle, all facing east, to the rising sun. And there were all the people, going about their business, laughing and talking and helping each other.

"My hut is better than yours," said Hare, "because it was built by everyone and everyone lives near it, where I can have my fun with them."

The people, who heard all of this, looked around and realized that it really is sweet to live together, sharing, helping, knowing each other. And that was Hare's first gift: the village.

Hyena lost his smile at this point. "Hmmmph! Well . . . you also promised a feast better than mine."

And all the people ran to get the food and drink that they had prepared. And because no one had to do it all, each could contribute what he or she cooked the best, so the feast had everyone's favorite foods. And that made everyone happy, which, of course, let the storytellers relax and tell their best stories. In time, just before anyone asked about Hare's second gift, he came out of his new hut dragging his hollow log and sticks.

"So far," he said, "this has been a pretty good feast, but I want to make it the best feast ever given. And it's also time for my second gift. Be quiet and listen."

With that, Hare picked up his sticks and began to tap on the log with them. At first he beat out a simple rhythm, and then he warmed to more and more complex rhythms. Soon the people began to twitch with the rhythm and sway and move. Suddenly Butterfly jumped up and began to swing her body and move in a circle around the fire, and before long everyone joined her, dancing to the rhythm of the drum Hare had invented and given to them.

Now sometimes folks argue about all of this. Some say that Hare really gave the people three gifts—the village, the drum, and music—while others claim that the music and the drum are really only one. But you know what I think? I think that it hardly matters, though I'm sure Hare enjoys the argument.

Sometimes

Sometimes,

When dawn begins to spread
Across the sky like melted butter and honey
And the air is trembling and still with waiting;
When the doves call out from the oaks
And my cat crawls on my chest and purrs
And kneads the covers like a nursing kitten;
When I hang like a drop of dew
On the cobweb spun between consciousness and sleep,
When I hang and quiver and slide slowly awake;
For just that moment of complete stillness,
I hear a music in my soul and I know
With the certainty of roses growing in the garden
    That the world holds out a promise of peace
    And it is my work to redeem the promise.

Sometimes,

When I climb in the hills and surprise
A deer or a bobcat or a hawk
Gliding and circling and hovering in the air before
    it dives;
When I stop and look over
The valleys and sip some water from my bottle
And rest in the green and glowing light;

For a moment, when the sun dances with the wind,
Free and laughing and filled with harmony
And joy, young and growing and bright;
For just that moment of fullness and knowledge,
I feel something touch my heart and I know
With the strength of stone and flowing water
    That we all touch each other and sing together
    And create the dancing peace of harmony.

The
Interdependent
Web of
All Existence

I want to begin my discussion of this last Principle with an account of how it was proposed, because its history is unique among the seven. Unitarian Universalists went through a study process for four years that culminated at the 1984 General Assembly with the proposal of a new statement of Unitarian Universalist Principles and in 1985 with the adoption of that statement. This process amounted to a dialogue between local congregations and a Unitarian Universalist Association Commission. The 1984 proposal contained versions of each of the first six Principles, but it did not directly mention interdependence. The concept was, perhaps, implicit in a number of other principles, especially the first concerning the inherent worth and dignity of every person, but even that one did not extend to non-humans. Many of us thought that there was something important missing, and some of us were prepared to vote against the proposal unless it were changed.

As the debate wore on and patience grew thin, the Reverend Paul L'Herrou stood up and proposed this seventh Principle. Some wordcrafting ensued, but because almost everyone agreed with it in substance, the final draft passed with few, if any, dissenting votes. A funny thing has happened since then. We appeal to these Principles for all sorts of things, from supporting social action projects to theological discussions and beyond. Of all seven, it is this last Principle that is appealed to by far the most often.

I was part of the group in 1984 that insisted on adding something about the interdependence of all. We got the idea from thinking about biology, especially ecology, and many of us specifically had in mind the justification of ecological action. One of the basic principles of ecology is that no living thing exists in isolation from its environment. Every creature and every species depends on every other for its existence, so that the elimination of a species necessarily weakens an environment and endangers the existence of all the remaining species, ours included. It is a law as inexorable as gravity.

Deeper reflection, however, reveals that this is a far more powerful statement than many of us ever imagined. The theology implicit in it is staggering. In spite of the fact that for Unitarian Universalists the primary unit of religion is the individual and the primary religious experience is the individual's ultimately intimate experience of meaning, depth, profundity, and beauty, none of us is isolated from our religious communities and the rest of creation. Again, the biological community is a very good model. The primary unit of life is the individual organism, yet no individual organism lives in isolation from its environment. As in the biological community, our spiritual lives are meaningless in isolation from the religious community.

Like many profound ideas, this is easy to state and grasp yet not easy to live. This idea is the core of Unitarian Universalist theology, more basic even than the inherent worth and dignity of all. It is in virtue of this interdependence that worth inheres to all. We could spend the rest of this book exploring this interdependency at the intellectual level, but I want to do something different. I want to explore what differences a commitment to this Principle would make in the lives that we actually live.

Think about the level of crime, violence, and despair that we see around us and ask yourself what would follow from this Principle. If we really are all interdependent, then would it not follow that despair anywhere in the world affects us? Would it not follow that crime in East Oakland, East Palo Alto, San Jose, Brooklyn, Washington, and anywhere else affects us? Would it not follow that violence in the home of our neighbor next door or across the street or on the next block affects us? And would it not follow that the idea of getting tough on crime, violence, drug trafficking, and so on also affects us and makes us hard and insensitive—tough?

Interdependence is an energy that flows in both directions. If the wolf is dependent on the caribou, then the caribou is also dependent on the wolf; if I am dependent on you, then you are also dependent on me. We cannot escape each other. When our government gets tough on crime, that hardness rebounds not only on criminals but on all of us. And when we raise the level of anxiety and despair among the poor by forgetting that they are real people who need help, then we raise our own level of anxiety, fear, and despair.

It is an old and universal theological doctrine. The Hindus and Buddhists call it karma. Jesus said, "That which you sow also shall you reap." The Taoists say, "Returning is the motion of the *Tao*." And folklore says, "What goes around, comes around." When we get stingy and greedy with people we do not know, that greed and stinginess rebounds on us and makes it easier for us to be greedy and stingy with each other. At a time when the gap between the wealthy and the poor is increasing, the middle class is feeling an increasing sense of financial insecurity and a culture of scarcity. As this culture of scarcity is growing, a culture of criticism is also growing. It is the dark side of interdependence.

If we treat some people critically and disdainfully, it becomes easier to treat others badly. Before long, what goes around comes around. Wagons begin to circle. Sides are chosen. Despair and anguish is heard, even among ourselves. And the fighting begins.

Do you want to stop—or even slow—the drug trade? Then begin by recognizing that we are all interdependent. If the addict depends on you, then you depend on the addict. Do you want to stop the drug trade? Then give the addict the same level of respect that you expect from the addict and work to make life without drugs more attractive than life addicted. Begin by making schools work. Begin by making it possible for poor parents to take meaningful jobs. Begin by supporting clean, bright, safe, and loving daycare. Begin by working for safe and humane prisons. Begin by affirming the lives of those who frighten you and threaten you and make you afraid. As my friend and colleague, Terry Sweetser, once remarked, "The best defense is a strong affirmation." What goes around, comes around.

There was a time in the history of Unitarian Universalism when we understood and acted on this idea. In 1939 rumors about the terrible treatment of Jews in Nazi Germany were beginning to be heard in America. A group of Unitarian ministers heard these rumors and they sent one of their number to Germany to find out the truth. He was appalled by what he found and when he returned to New York, he and his group founded the Unitarian Service Committee. Their mission was to help Jews in occupied Europe, and they did, sometimes at great risk to themselves. Why did they do this? Because they understood, even if they may have articulated it differently, that we are all interdependent. They understood that what happens to defenseless Jews in Germany happens to all of us.

What happens to defenseless children in the homes of our land happens to all of us. The battered, the abused, the neglected, the poor, the addicted, the unloved children are not only our children. They are us. Are they helped by a hardened heart? Or a softened heart? We are interdependent; what we say and do about and to others, we say and do to ourselves. And are we helped by a hardened heart or a softened heart?

This is not the place for an extended discussion of the crisis level of despair and rage that alarms so many of us, but I cannot conclude this discussion of interdependence without noticing it. It is not an essentially economic crisis or a military one or even a crisis of government. Any crises we may have are symptoms of something far deeper, far more important, and therefore far harder to deal with. We are in the midst of a cultural spiritual crisis occasioned by the fact that we have lost sight of this seventh Unitarian Universalist Principle.

One of the best images of what our culture has become is the actor Zero Mostel playing Pontius Pilate. Jesus is brought before him and he asks what the man teaches. A centurion says that Jesus tells people to love their enemies. A sneer of derisive laughter explodes from Pilate, and he says, "Love your enemies?!" as if the idea is pure insanity. What goes around, comes around. If the politics of the 1980s and early 1990s was the politics of selfishness and greed, and it sowed anger, jealousy, and resentful despair among the poor, then the harvest is anger, jealousy, and resentful despair among us as the poor adopt the selfishness they were shown.

Do you see how powerful this idea of interdependence is? It has to do with justifying ecological action, to be sure, but it is far more than that. It is also about how we live our lives and treat each other and conceive of our communities. It is about how we are woven into life's web. It is also about how biology becomes a meta-

phor for the depth of life where meaning and fulfill-
ment and love dwell.

Consider this passage from D. H. Lawrence's novel,
The Rainbow, in which he describes the rural people who
lived in a small village:

> . . . heaven and earth was teaming around them,
> and how should this cease? They felt the rush of
> the sap in spring, they knew the wave which can-
> not halt, but every year throws forward the seed
> to begetting, and, falling back, leaves the young-
> born on the earth. They knew the intercourse
> between heaven and earth, sunshine drawn into
> the breast and bowels, the rain sucked up in the
> daytime, nakedness that comes under the wind in
> autumn, showing bird's nests no longer worth hid-
> ing. Their lives and interrelations were such; feel-
> ing the pulse and body of the soil that opened to
> their furrow for the grain and became smooth and
> supple after their ploughing and clung to their feet
> with a weight that pulled like desire, lying hard
> and unresponsive when the crops were to be shorn
> way. The young corn waved and was silken, and
> the lustre slid along the limbs of [those] who saw
> it. They took the udder of the cows, the cows
> yielded milk and pulsed against [their] hands, the
> pulse of the blood of the teats of the cows beat
> against the pulse of the hand. . . . They mounted
> their horses, and held life between the grip of their

knees, they harnessed their horse at the wagon, and, with hand on bridle rings, drew the horses after their will. In autumn the partridges whirred up, birds in flocks blew like spray across the fallow, rooks appeared on the gray, watery heavens and flew cawing into the winter.

This passage is not just about the characters; it's about us. It's a metaphor that points to our interconnected depths where we live out the meaning of our lives.

This is the real cash value. We are interconnected, interdependent. This is simply so, as true religiously and spiritually as it is biologically. Since it is true, the minute we forget it and try to live as if we are autonomous units, looking after our own without concern for how our lives affect the lives of others, we lose sight of any chance to bring genuine meaning and joy and even love into our living.

It is not getting tough or trying to shut ourselves away from the criminals, the poor, and the suffering that will bring us security. It is opening our hearts and reaching out to them and helping them to build strong and meaningful lives. It is loving our neighbors as ourselves and loving our enemies. It is sowing the seeds of joy and happiness. It is dispelling hatred with love. If what goes around comes around, doesn't it make sense for us to send love around, love and help and generosity and kindness and understanding and a gentle, healing, and helping hand? That's what I want to come around to me, so that is what I try to send around.

How Spider Woman Created the World

There are many stories about how the world was created, stories that range from scientific accounts to mythology. I want to tell you a myth. It won't tell you what happened, but it might tell you about how to live in this wonderful world, for that is why people tell myths.

Way, way back, a long time ago, before there was a universe, Spider Woman went wandering up and down, looking for something. She was lonely and wanted company, but there was no company, for she was alone. All there was, all that she could find, was a huge mountain. Some say that this was Mt. Tamalpais, and others think it was a mountain in the Black Hills. Still others say it was Mt. Zion, or maybe it was in the Himalayas, Tibet, or Mt. Kilimanjaro. It doesn't matter which mountain it was. She went up on this mountain and sat down to think. Suddenly she had an idea. One thing everyone knows about Spider Woman is that she is the Weaver. And so she decided to set up her loom on top of the mountain. She strung up the yarn for the warp and it took her a long time, for she wanted this weaving to be something special and very long and beautiful. And when she got the loom set up, she took up her shuttle and began to weave.

And as she wove, something amazing happened.

Every time one thread crossed another, a star appeared, and before long she had woven thousands and thousands of stars into her weaving, and each one was tied to every other one in the web. Then she stopped and looked at it. It shone and sparkled and was very beautiful. But it was not quite what she wanted, so she decided that she would do a little more with this web of stars. She chose one star that happened to have some planets circling around it. And she chose one of those planets that had bright blue oceans and sparkling white clouds, and set up her loom again, right there on that planet. And she began to weave again.

This time as she wove, whenever one thread crossed another, a living thing appeared. She wove roses and pansies and carnations into this world. She wove fruit trees and nut trees and great redwoods. She wove all manner of birds and fish and insects into her web. She wove deer and buffalo and coyotes into it and all of the animals. And every one of these living things was connected to each other thing in her weaving. Then she stopped weaving to look at it. It was very beautiful and very full. Yet it was still not finished. There was still something missing, so she started to weave yet a third time.

This time when she wove, the crossing threads created human beings, men and women and children, all of us. And each human being that she wove into her Great Web was connected to every other thing, to the other animals, to the plants and trees and flowers, to the mountains and seas and deserts, even to the distant stars. Every human being—and indeed everything that Spider Woman wove into her Great Web—is connected to every other thing. And it is all beautiful and sacred. And you know, because every day someone is born and every day a new flower opens somewhere and a tree sprouts and a new animal is born, Spider Woman must still be weaving.

The Rain

The sky is filled and gray and black
With clouds left from this morning's rain.
And mists rise from dark puddles
And long rivers that flow slowly
Through the forest. And rain begins to fall
Again, like night falling through the afternoon,
Sifting through forests, settling on rivers,
Swirling around the long, greening hills
That stand as silent as rocks in the river.

The whispering, patient rain slides
Through new leaves and seems
To speak like dreams and faint glimpses
Of something not quite visible,
A face or a voice or the echo of a music
So faint and distant, so suggested and hinted
That I'm not even sure it's there.
But whether I look through rain or leaves,
It's there and gone and back again,
Whispering, hinting, powerful yet distant.

What is this constant presence, this music,
This voice that I can't quite hear?
Whose face is it that hides
In the raw leaves of spring

And the rising, swirling mists?
What is this strength, this power, this love
That wells upward like sparkling water
And fills my heart like falling rain,
And stands as rich and silent as the hills?
It is the echo of the echo of the memory of
    mystery.

And rain continues to fall through the night.